To Mary

ENJOY THE RECORDER

A comprehensive method for group, individual and self tuition

– by –

BRIAN BONSOR

DESCANT TUTOR BOOK I

Edition 11464

Mainz · London · Madrid · New York · Paris · Tokyo · Toronto

© 1981 SCHOTT & CO. LTD., LONDON
Edition No. 11464

Text setting by: Furlonger Phototext Ltd., Bournemouth
Illustrations by: Derrick Smith, Poole
Design by: Derek Carmichael, Corfe Mullen

Printed in Germany

Foreword

The best way to learn any instrument is to have lessons from a good, experienced teacher. Although, happily, the number of such teachers is constantly growing, the recorder is still frequently taught by enthusiastic but inexperienced teachers and many players start by teaching themselves.

This series of books sets out to help learners of all ages in all three situations. Experienced teachers, who may choose to disregard much of the text as personal demonstration is always clearer than the written word, will find exercises and fine tunes a-plenty to support their own method at each stage. The less experienced will benefit from many valuable teaching hints culled from long experience and may rely on the books to lead to a sound playing technique and a mastery of simple notation.

Those learning by themselves — and I started in this way — are urged to work carefully and systematically through the books, taking plenty of time to assimilate each point before moving on. For them, without the personal model provided by a live teacher, it is vitally important to listen as often as possible to fine players, in person or on record, so that they have in their mind's ear a clear notion of the kind of sound they would like to produce.

But however they start, I can only wish that all who use these books will derive as much pleasure and musical satisfaction and gain as many lasting and valued friendships as I have through this most subtle, delightful and sociable of instruments.

Brian Bonsor

Know Your Recorder

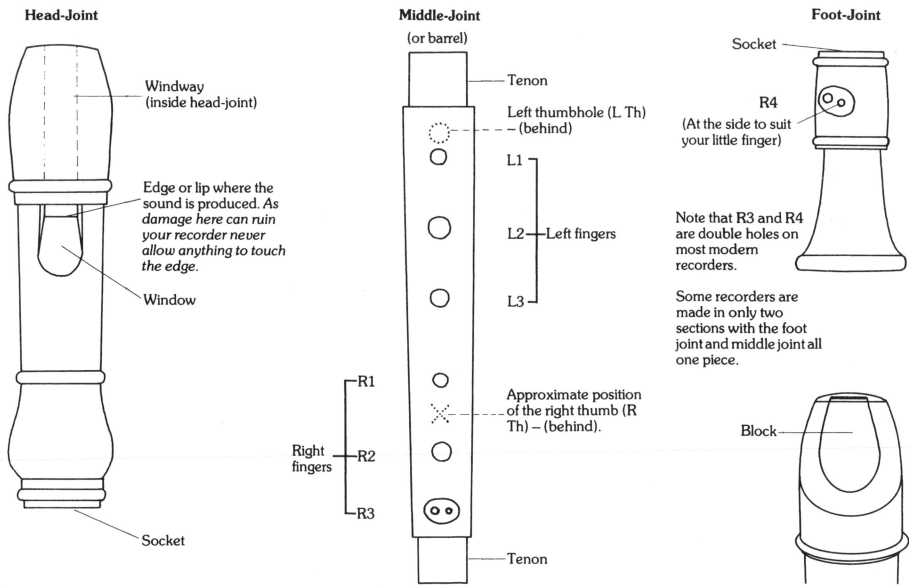

Head-Joint

Windway
(inside head-joint)

Edge or lip where the
sound is produced. *As
damage here can ruin
your recorder never
allow anything to touch
the edge.*

Window

Socket

Middle-Joint
(or barrel)

Tenon

Left thumbhole (L Th)
– (behind)

L1

L2 — Left fingers

L3

R1

Right
fingers — R2

R3

Approximate position
of the right thumb (R
Th) – (behind).

Tenon

Foot-Joint

Socket

R4
(At the side to suit
your little finger)

Note that R3 and R4
are double holes on
most modern
recorders.

Some recorders are
made in only two
sections with the foot
joint and middle joint all
one piece.

Block

Handling Your Recorder

Treat your recorder well and it will repay your kindness.

Assembling your recorder: (a) take a joint in each hand; (b) insert the tenon of the middle joint into the socket and slowly *twist* the joints into place. A smear of suitable grease on cork-lined or plastic tenons will help. **Never push the tenon straight into its socket: damage can easily result.**

Warming your recorder: warm your recorder *gently* before playing by holding particularly the head-joint in the hands or under the arm. Trouser pockets are also useful but guard against tiny pieces of fluff or other matter entering the windway.

Never warm a recorder near a fire or radiator or in direct sunlight.

After playing: always dry out your recorder with a soft *fluffless* cloth (e.g. a cotton handkerchief). Be wary of the mops sold for swabbing out recorders. Too many deposit fluff inside the instrument and do more harm than good. If you have such a mop, covering it with a thin cotton handkerchief makes an *effective* swab. Make sure that the tip of the wire stem of the mop is protected in some way or damage to the block may result, especially in wooden recorders.

Finally, treat *music* (including this book!) with equal care. Never fold or bend it, and always carry it in a suitable case, or between stiff covers, protected from the weather.

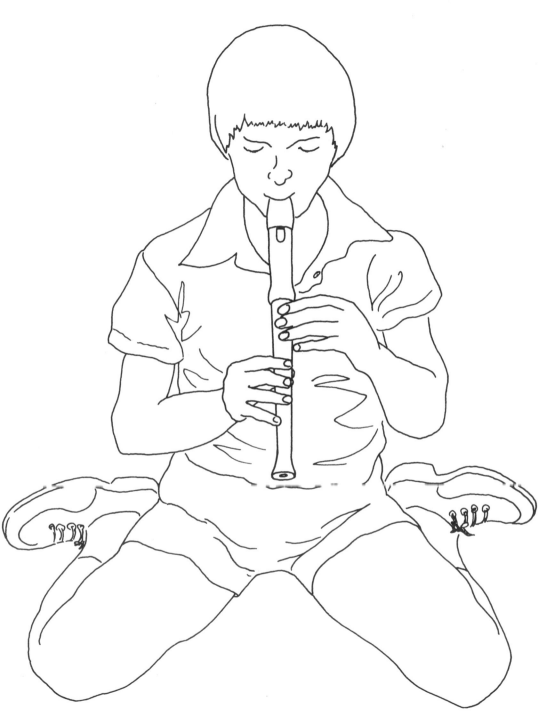

Making the First Sound

Holding your recorder as shown, put the tip of the mouthpiece (about ¼" – 6mm) between your lips and blow a steady, but *gentle,* stream of air through the instrument. *Your teeth must not touch the mouthpiece.*

If the sound is harsh and shrill – blow more gently.

If the sound is weak and wavery – blow *slightly* more strongly until your breath seems to fill the instrument.

The sound should remain steady throughout:

and not

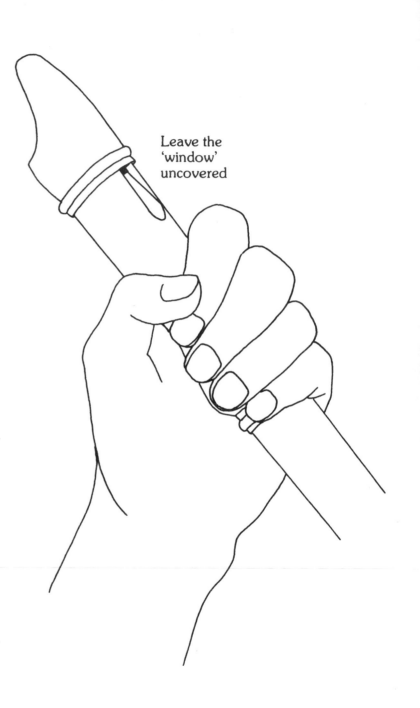

Leave the 'window' uncovered

Starting a Note

To give the sound a clean, clear start:

(a) take the recorder away from your mouth and say the sound 'doo', holding the 'oo' sound for about five seconds;

(b) now say – 'doo-doo-doo-doo-doo', holding each 'doo' for about a second, and feel the tip of your tongue touch the hard, crinkly ridge above your upper front teeth;

(c) now, *blowing out continuously (this is most important),* whisper 'doo-doo-doo-doo-doo' and you will hear a faint sound as your tongue pulls back from the ridge;

(d) now repeat (c) as you blow through your recorder with a *steady* breath to produce a series of notes. **You are now tonguing** – and, for the time being, every note you play will be tongued.

If your tonguing produces little explosions of sound, relax and use your tongue more gently.

Ending a Note

To end a note neatly, bring your tongue back up to the ridge behind your teeth and this will prevent any air from passing down the recorder.

6

Now that you can start and stop sounds neatly, try making sounds of different lengths.
As you play, count a steady 1, 2, 3, 4 in your head.

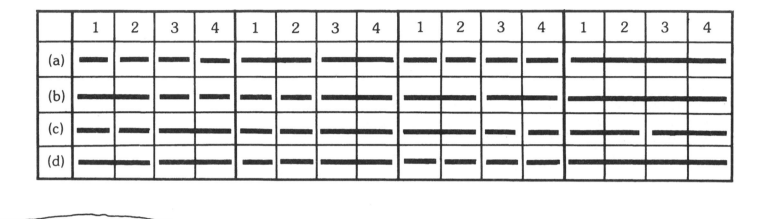

	1	2	3	4	1	2	3	4	1	2	3	4	1	2	3	4
(a)	—	—	—	—	—	—	—	—	—	—	—	—	—	—	—	—
(b)	—		—	—	—	—	—	—	—	—	—	—	—		—	—
(c)	—	—	—	—	—	—	—	—	—	—	—	—	—	—	—	—
(d)	—	—	—	—	—	—	—	—	—	—	—	—	—	—	—	—

Clearing a Blocked Recorder

After playing for a short time, your recorder may sound either muffled, strangely out of tune or even completely blocked. The cause in each case is moisture in the windway which can be easily removed by laying a finger gently *across* (**not into !**) the window and blowing once, sharply, through the mouthpiece.

If the mouthpiece starts to clog whilst you are playing, a quick suck will usually clear it temporarily.

Using your Fingers

Look at the diagram on the right and note –

1. that the left hand is used *above* the right;

2. that each finger covers only one hole and *never* moves to any other. (The small double holes like R3/R4 count, meantime, as one hole.)
Fingers not in use are held directly above their own holes, about 1″ (25mm) away;

3. that the left hand little finger (L4) is the only finger not used;

4. the position of the right thumb – at the back, midway between R1 and R2 i.e. almost exactly halfway between the thumbhole and the end of the instrument – which will be shown in all fingering charts by X. To support the instrument the thumb is placed here *even when the right hand fingers are not being used*. **Never allow your right hand to slip down and grasp the foot-joint.**

Finger-holes are covered by the **pads** of the fingers – **not** the tips. As a check, put your left thumb (L Th) on the hole at the back and your left fingers on the three holes nearest the mouthpiece and press down firmly. You will feel the edges of the holes dig into your fingers, making little mounds which will clearly show if the hole has been properly covered. Now compare your fingers with this diagram:

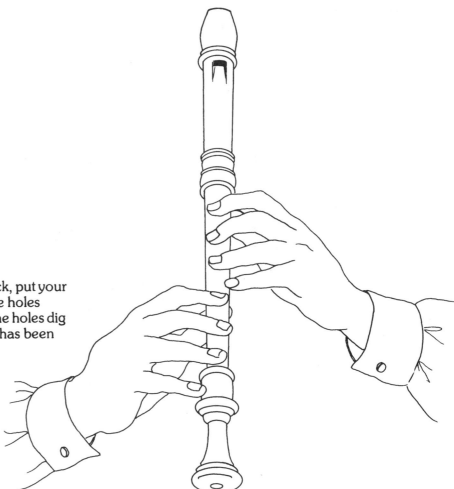

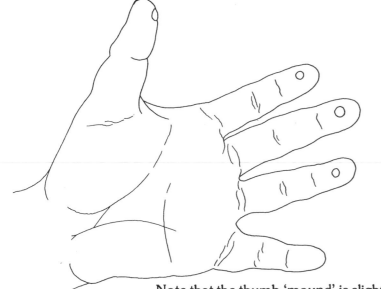

This (modified) drawing, taken from a French recorder tutor of 1707 by Jacques Hotteterre, is still one of the best illustrations of good hand positions. *Note particularly the position of the right thumb.*

In playing position, the fingers are only slightly arched. (Picking up a pencil from a table puts the fingers in roughly the correct position.)

Note that the thumb 'mound' is slightly more to the side than those on the fingers.

The First Real Notes

Check: that the fingerholes (except R4) are in a straight line below the window.

Prop up this book, preferably on a music or desk stand, at a height which allows you to play without stooping. *Playing with music on your knees, flat on a table or on too low a stand may restrict your breathing and lead you into bad habits.*

Sit (or stand) up straight. Hold your recorder, *without gripping,* at an angle of about 45° to your body, keeping your elbows near to, *but not touching,* your sides. Fingers, hands and arms should feel comfortably relaxed.

To play

B

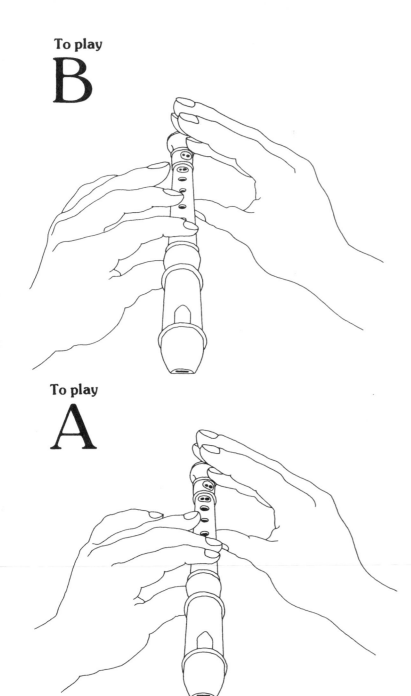

Now:

(a) put your left thumb (L Th) on the hole at the back;

(b) put your left first finger (L1) on the hole nearest the mouthpiece;

(c) put your right thumb (R Th) under the instrument at X. Hold your other fingers about 1″ (25mm) above their own holes.

(d) remember to tongue.

(e) blow gently and play a 'B'!

(f) play another – and another, *tonguing each time.*

Keep the sounds steady!

Finally, practise laying down and picking up your recorder to play B so that your fingers – and your right thumb – learn to find their places quickly.

The instructions in (a), (b) and (c) can be clearly shown by a simple diagram:

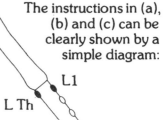

To play

A

When you can play B successfully, add L2 and, if all the holes are still properly sealed, the sound will change to the note A.

Practise raising and lowering L2 *without moving the finger and thumb already down.*

Keep your finger movements small and neat, lifting the fingers only an inch (25mm) or so above the recorder.

To play

G

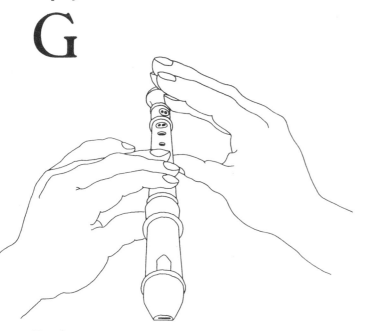

To play

E

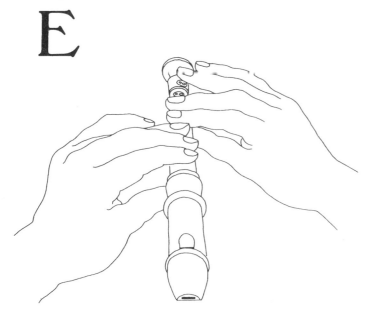

Finger A and add L3. Push L3 across until you feel the hole in the centre of the pad. Check that L Th, L1 and L2 have not moved from their holes and that R Th is still in position.

Blow and tongue gently.

Enjoy Yourself!

Play around with the three notes B, A and G until your fingers find the holes easily. Remember to tongue; play notes of different lengths, making up your own melodies; and take particular care always to produce a pleasant sound.

Using the Right Hand

To help set the position of the right hand, finger G and add R1 and R2. This is the fingering for low E. Blow and tongue *very gently*.

Practise playing from G to E and back, raising and lowering R1 and R2 *absolutely together,* and dropping your breath a little as you add the right hand fingers.

Training your "Mind's Ear"

Although we shall not meet low E again until page 32, carry on using it (and, so, your right hand) while playing back tunes played to you by your teacher or friends and by inventing tunes for them to play back to you. This 'echo' game will prove really useful as each new note is introduced throughout this book.

Other helpful games are (1) to listen to a tune without seeing it fingered and **sing** it back to the letter names of the notes (you can then play it, too, if you like); and (2) to watch a tune being fingered but not blown and sing it back to the letter names (i.e. without having heard it).

11

Learning to Read Music

When you feel happy about blowing, tonguing and fingering B, A, G and E, move on and we shall see how the first three look in musical notation.

First you should know that music is written on a set of five lines called a *staff* or *stave*.

Descant recorder music has a *treble clef* (𝄞) at the beginning of each line

which fixes the names of the lines and spaces as —

LINES   SPACES

Choose one of the following phrases to help you to remember the names of the lines (or make one up for yourself!):

Every **G**ood **B**oy **D**eserves **F**avour (or **F**un)
Every **G**reen **B**us **D**rives **F**ast
Elephants **G**o **B**ackwards **D**own **F**ire-escapes

The spaces spell **FACE.**

Lines and spaces are counted *from the bottom up* i.e.
E is the first line: F' is the fifth.
F is the first space: E' is the fourth.

B is therefore on the third line and A is in the second space.

12

Now Read and Play

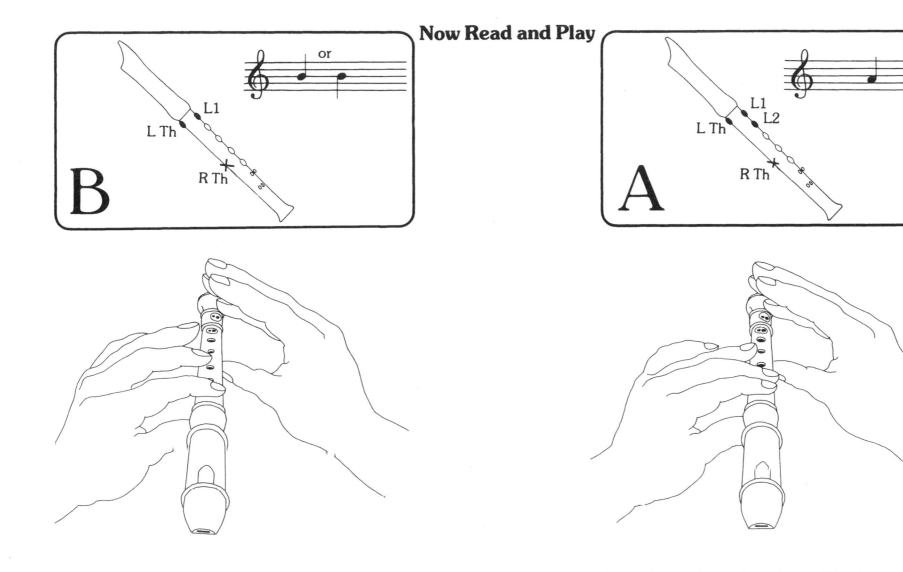

Like you, all the music in this book has a regular *pulse*. For the time being this *pulse* or *beat* will be represented by —

A Crotchet (or Quarter-note) :   ♩ or ♩

A sound two pulses or beats long will be shown by —

A Minim (or Half-Note) :   ♩ or ♩

Look at the music and try to remember that —
B is "on a line" (i.e. the line passes through the note-head): A is "in a space" (i.e. the note-head fills the space).

1. Our First Tune Uses Only B

Check: 1. that the fingerholes are under the window.
2. that your left hand is *above* your right.
3. that your right thumb is in position.
4. that your unused fingers are clear of the holes.

Remember, too, to tongue *every* note.

* ∨ = take a breath

2. This Tune Uses A and B.

Before you play it – and all the tunes that follow – rest your mouthpiece on your chin
and say or, better still, sing aloud the names of the notes as you silently finger them at
the speed you hope to play them.

3. Which note does this tune use? How long is the first note? Are you still tonguing every note?

4. Which notes does this tune use? Name and finger them as before.

5. On which notes does this tune begin and end? Name and finger all the notes.

The small lines drawn from the top to the bottom of the stave are
bar-lines, and the distance between two bar-lines is one *bar.*

How many bars of music are there in each of tunes 1 – 5?

←— ONE BAR —→

Barline   Barline

6.

Each tune ends with two bar-lines drawn close together.
Musicians call this a "double bar".

⊛ **Enjoy the Recorder Book 1A contains piano accompaniments
to all tunes except those marked □**

A New Note

So far each tune has had **4 beats in each bar**. The next few tunes will have only 3, and will use a new note 3 beats long.

The Dotted Minim (or Dotted Half-Note)

Learn this rule: A dot *after* a note *adds on* half the value of the note.

We shall be meeting other dotted notes later.

Remember to sing the names of the notes as you finger them, *before* playing each tune.

7.

8.

9.

10.

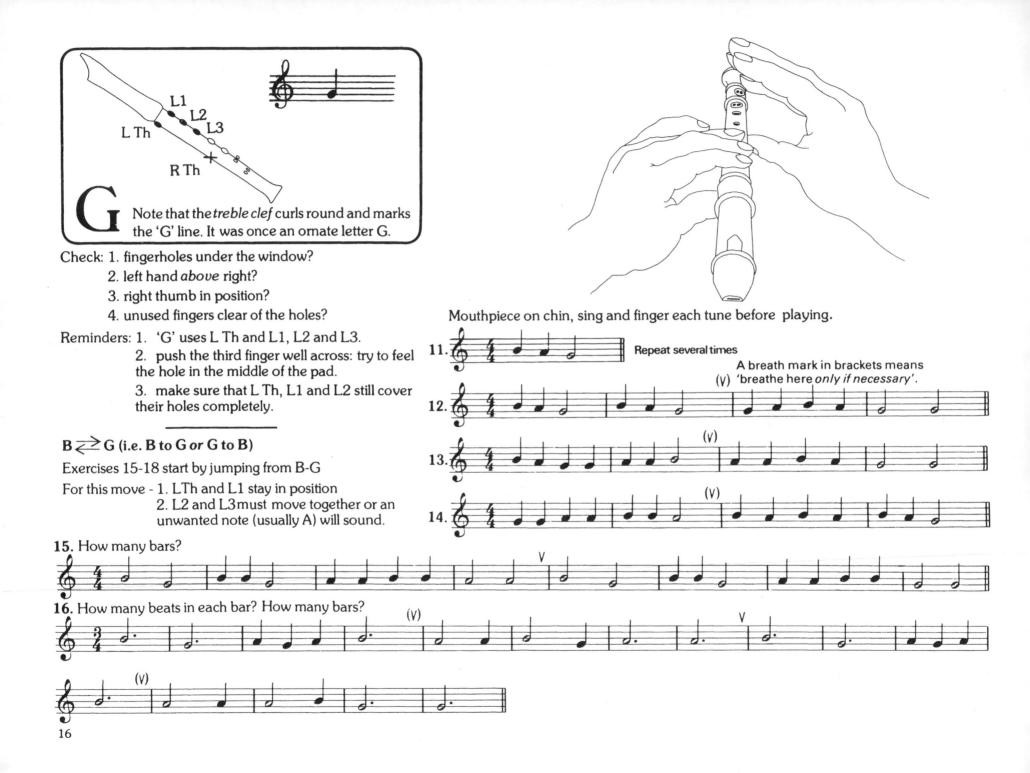

G Note that the *treble clef* curls round and marks the 'G' line. It was once an ornate letter G.

Check: 1. fingerholes under the window?

2. left hand *above* right?

3. right thumb in position?

4. unused fingers clear of the holes?

Reminders: 1. 'G' uses L Th and L1, L2 and L3.

2. push the third finger well across: try to feel the hole in the middle of the pad.

3. make sure that L Th, L1 and L2 still cover their holes completely.

B ⇄ G (i.e. B to G *or* G to B)

Exercises 15-18 start by jumping from B-G

For this move - 1. LTh and L1 stay in position

2. L2 and L3 must move together or an unwanted note (usually A) will sound.

15. How many bars?

16. How many beats in each bar? How many bars?

Mouthpiece on chin, sing and finger each tune before playing.

11. Repeat several times

A breath mark in brackets means
(V) 'breathe here *only if necessary*'.

12.

13.

14.

17.

The Tie

A curved line joining the heads of two notes *on the same line or in the same space* is called a TIE. The second note is not tongued and its beat value is added to that of the first.

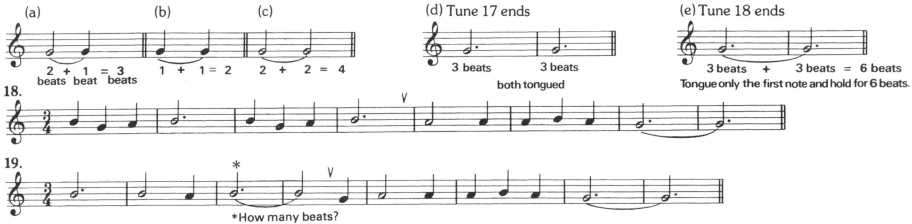

(a) 2 + 1 = 3
beats beat beats

(b) 1 + 1 = 2

(c) 2 + 2 = 4

(d) Tune 17 ends
3 beats 3 beats
both tongued

(e) Tune 18 ends
3 beats + 3 beats = 6 beats
Tongue only the first note and hold for 6 beats.

18.

19.

*How many beats?

Musical Terms

Musicians all over the world use certain Italian words to describe how music is to be performed. Some of these words will be introduced gradually from now on and will be explained the first time they are used. Try to memorise them as you meet them but, if you should forget, you will find them all listed on **page 98.**

Loud and Soft

Perhaps the most commonly used terms are those referring to loudness and softness:

f – short for *forte* meaning loud

p – short for *piano* meaning soft

m – short for *mezzo* meaning medium, but often translated as 'moderately'.

Hence:

mf – mezzo forte – moderately loud

mp – mezzo piano – moderately soft

You are now ready to play the first concert piece – "Drifting Along". Turn to page 91 and enjoy your first full-length piece.

An oval note without a stem is a —

Semibreve (Whole Note)

𝗈

Hold the sound for *4 beats*.

20. The piano will help you count the semibreves.

Some useful musical shorthand

1. 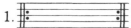 Repeat the music between the dots. If only the *second* dots and double bar appear repeat from the beginning of the piece.

2. 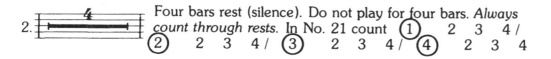 Four bars rest (silence). Do not play for four bars. *Always count through rests.* In No. 21 count ① 2 3 4 / ② 2 3 4 / ③ 2 3 4 / ④ 2 3 4

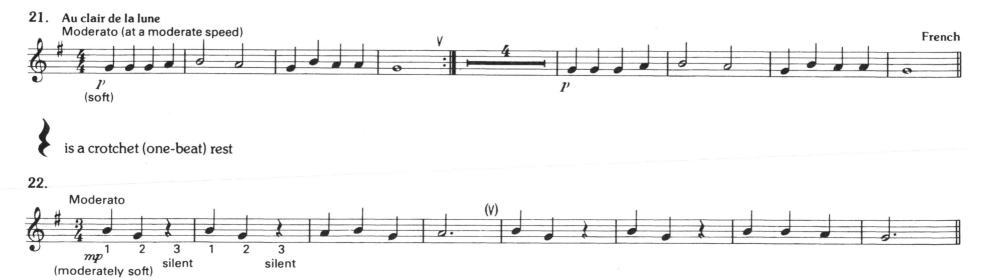

21. Au clair de la lune
Moderato (at a moderate speed)

French

p
(soft)

p

❴ is a crotchet (one-beat) rest

22.
Moderato

mp
(moderately soft)

1 2 3   1 2 3
   silent   silent

18

The joined notes in tunes 23-26 are —

Quavers (Eighth Notes)

♪ or ♫

One quaver standing alone has a hooked tail. Two quavers are joined together by a straight bar and together take up the time of one crotchet.

$$\text{♫} = \text{♩}$$

$$\tfrac{1}{2} + \tfrac{1}{2} = 1$$

A quaver rest is written: ♪

Counting quavers

To count quavers say "and" after the beat number:

Sing a song of sixpence, a pocket full of rye

1 and 2 and 3 4 and 1 and 2 and 3 4

Rhythm exercises

Clap each exercise twice, counting aloud the first time and in your head the second.

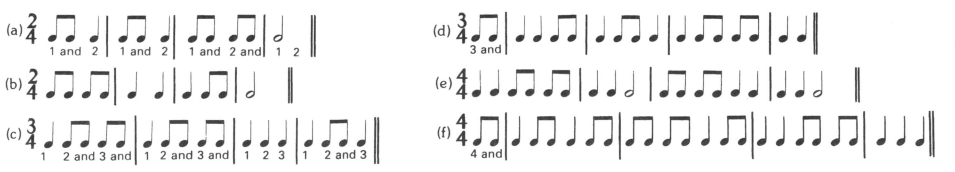

Now, using B, A, G or E, play each rhythm entirely on one note:
then, using all four notes, try to make up tunes to fit the rhythms.

Tunes with quavers

23. Here's a health unto His Majesty (part only)

Allegretto (fairly fast and lively)   (V)   English

mf (moderately loud)

24. "Who's dat yonder?" (Slightly altered)

Moderato   Negro Spiritual

mf   original

25. Spannenlanger Hansel

German

Andante (At a moderate (walking) pace)   *

mp   *mp*

*Count the 4 bars rest: If there were 6 bars rest, how would you continue to count?

① 2 ② 2 ③ 2 ④ 2

26. It's me, O Lord.

Not too fast   V   (V)   Negro Spiritual

mf

A new rhythm:

Remember that when two notes are tied,
only the first is tongued and the beat value of the
second is added to it.

Count: ① 2 (and) ③ 4 (and) ① ② ③ 4   and tongue only the circled counts.

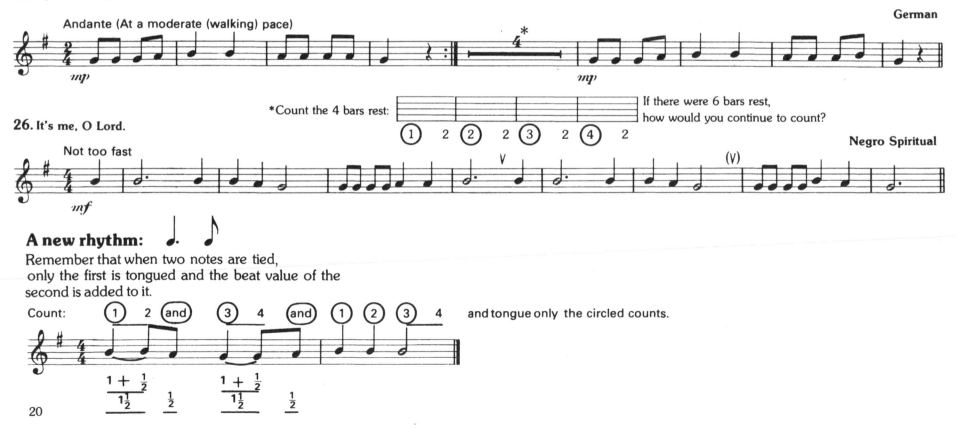

$1 + \frac{1}{2}$ $1 + \frac{1}{2}$

$1\frac{1}{2}$ $\frac{1}{2}$ $1\frac{1}{2}$ $\frac{1}{2}$

27a Merrily we roll along

As a dot after a note adds on half the value of the note, ♩. is also 1½ beats
(♩. = 1 + ½), and tune 27a could be written –

This is clearer and more usual.

27b

28. Andante

29. Moderato

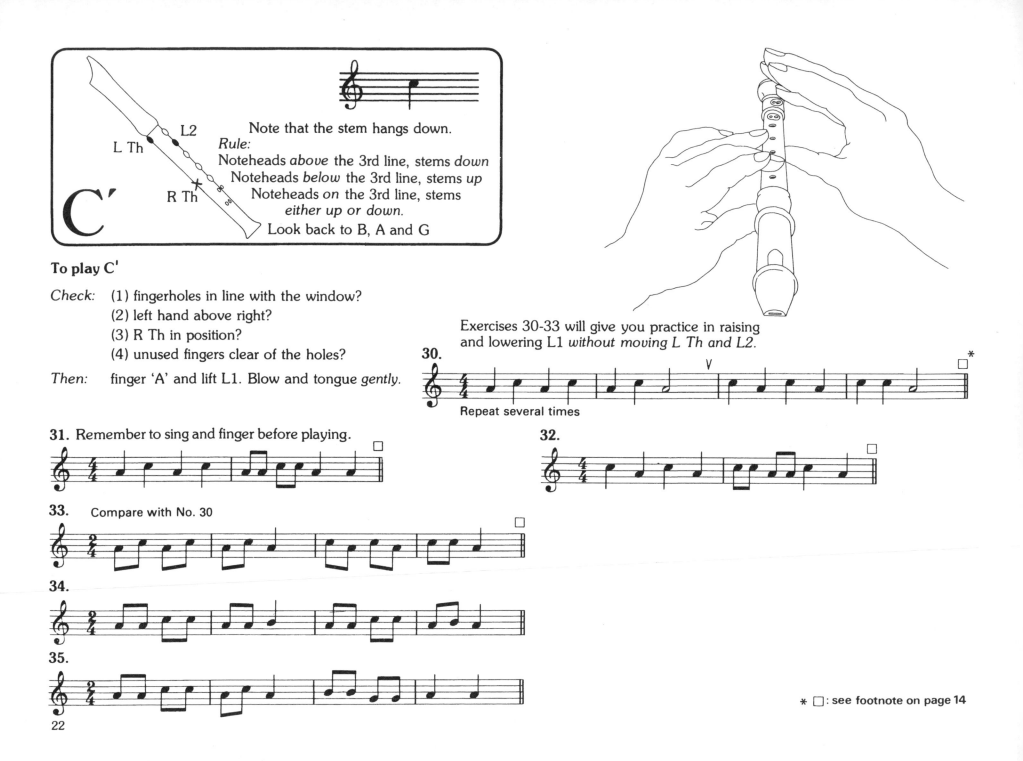

Note that the stem hangs down.
Rule:
Noteheads *above* the 3rd line, stems *down*
Noteheads *below* the 3rd line, stems *up*
Noteheads *on* the 3rd line, stems
either up or down.
Look back to B, A and G

C'

To play C'

Check: (1) fingerholes in line with the window?
(2) left hand above right?
(3) R Th in position?
(4) unused fingers clear of the holes?

Then: finger 'A' and lift L1. Blow and tongue *gently.*

Exercises 30-33 will give you practice in raising
and lowering L1 *without moving L Th and L2.*

30.

Repeat several times

31. Remember to sing and finger before playing.

32.

33. Compare with No. 30

34.

35.

* ☐ : see footnote on page 14

22

C'⇄B: If an unwanted note (A) sounds between C' and B, L2 has stayed down too long: if between B and C', L1 is the lazy finger. 'Outgoing' fingers (i.e. fingers being *raised*) are often slow. Always give them special thought.

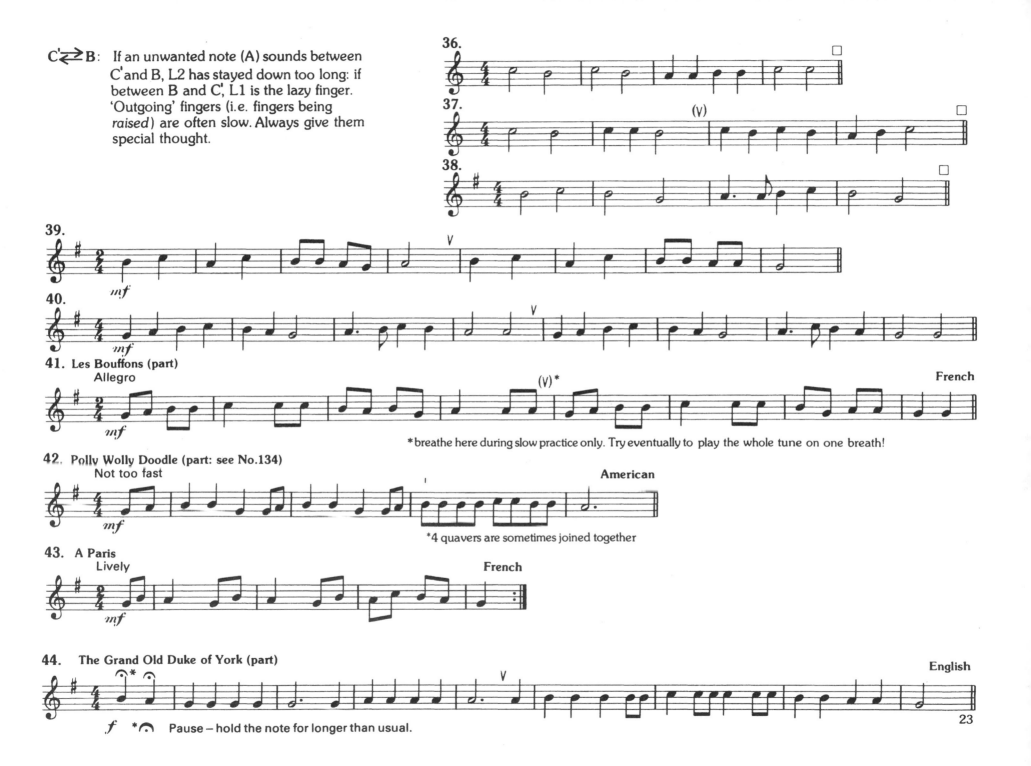

36.

37. (V)

38.

39. *mf*

40. *mf*

41. Les Bouffons (part)
Allegro (V)* French
mf

*breathe here during slow practice only. Try eventually to play the whole tune on one breath!

42. Polly Wolly Doodle (part: see No.134)
Not too fast American
mf

*4 quavers are sometimes joined together

43. A Paris
Lively French
mf

44. The Grand Old Duke of York (part)
English
f * ⌢ Pause – hold the note for longer than usual.

23

C⇄G : Keeping L Th and L2 in position, practise lifting and lowering L1 and L3
    together. As the 3rd fingers of both hands tend to be lazy, pay special attention to L3.

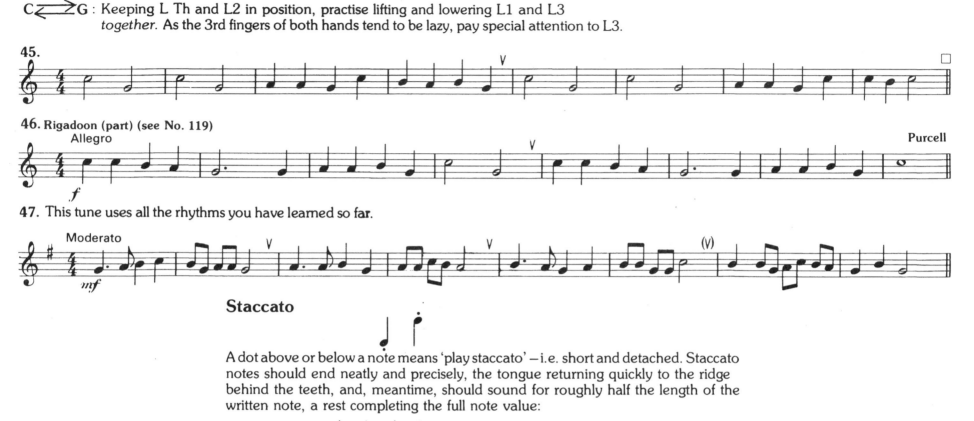

46. Rigadoon (part) (see No. 119)

47. This tune uses all the rhythms you have learned so far.

Staccato

A dot above or below a note means 'play staccato' – i.e. short and detached. Staccato notes should end neatly and precisely, the tongue returning quickly to the ridge behind the teeth, and, meantime, should sound for roughly half the length of the written note, a rest completing the full note value:

Avoid the common mistake of tonguing staccato notes too forcibly.

Tongue normally and *simply shorten the end of the note.*

Concert Piece No. 2 – 'March' – on p. 92 gives further practice in staccato playing.
Keep the staccato notes short and precise, tonguing crisply *but lightly.* Turn to it now.

Recorders are made in many different sizes. The four shown here – from left to right, **descant**, **bass** (note the crook through which the player blows), **tenor** and **treble** – are those most often used, but the tiny **sopranino** (smaller and therefore higher pitched than your descant) and the **great bass** (a larger and deeper bass with a longer crook) are also fairly common nowadays. Even smaller and larger recorders exist but are still comparatively rare.

Although all recorders share the same basic fingering pattern, they divide into two main groups according to whether their lowest note is C (descant, tenor, great bass) or F (sopranino, treble, bass). Once you can play both a C and an F instrument (usually descant and treble) you will be able to move easily to any other recorder in normal use – though to play bass and great bass you will have to learn to read from the **bass clef**:

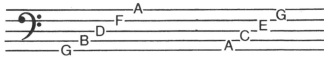

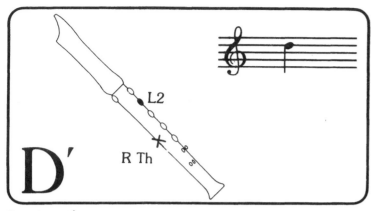

D' L2 R Th

To play D':

1. Carry out the usual checks
2. Finger C' and take off L Th – *not too far:* $\frac{1}{2}$in. (13mm) – 1in. (25mm) is enough.
3. *Blow and tongue gently.* This is especially important with D' which can be blown out of tune more easily than any other note on the descant recorder.

Exercise 50 (a) – C'⇌D'

Blow and tongue gently. L2 stays down throughout.

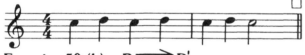

Exercise 50 (b) – B⇌D'

Like B⇌C', this move needs careful practice. Unwanted sounds often occur between B and D'.

If **A** sounds: *L1* and *L Th* have not moved off quickly enough.

If **C'** sounds: *L Th* has not moved off quickly enough.

If **C'** *sharp* (see p. 66) sounds: *L1* has not moved off quickly enough.

Exercise 50 (c) – A⇌D'

L2 stays down throughout: Move L Th and L1 *together*.

Exercise 50 (d) – G ⇄ D′

L2 stays down throughout: move L Th, L1 and L3 *together.*

51. Repeat Exercises 50 (a) (b) (c) and (d) many times.

52.

Tunes Giving Practice from C ⇄ D′ and B ⇄ D′ (Exercises 50 (a) and (b) above)

53. "Now the day is over" (Tune: Eudoxia)

Legato (smoothly): play each note for its full length before gently tonguing the next.

S. Baring-Gould

Are you still singing and fingering each tune before playing?

54. "Winter goodbye"

German

Moderato

p legato
(soft and smooth)

(get louder)   (get softer)

55. Ode to Joy (from the 9th Symphony)(part)

Beethoven

56. "His Rest" (part)

Giles Farnaby

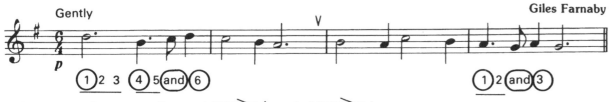

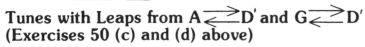

Tunes with Leaps from A⇄D′ and G⇄D′
(Exercises 50 (c) and (d) above)

57. Jingle Bells

J. Pierpont

58. Russian Tune

59. The Bee

Moderato

German

60. Dansons la capucine

Allegro   French
(V)

Although the double bar and repeat dots at the beginning of this tune are not strictly
necessary (see page 18), repeats at the beginning of a tune are sometimes printed this way.

61. Goe from my window (Adapted)

Slowly   Anon (English)

62. One man went to mow

Brightly   English

63. Oranges and lemons (part)

Not too fast   English

64. La Volta (part)

Allegretto   William Byrd

65. When the Saints go marchin' in

Tempo di marcia (in march time)   American

Tunes with Quaver Rests — ♪ (½-beat silence)

66. Wiegenlied (Lullaby)
Andante · German

67. Andante

You are now ready for Concert Piece No. 3 — "Beginners' Beguine", a piece in Latin-American style — on p. 93. Friends who play treble recorder or percussion can join you in this.

The Slur

The slur is a curved line similar to the tie (p. 17) but affecting two or more notes of *different* pitch (i.e. on different lines and spaces). Tongue only the first note and, *while still blowing continuously,* make all the others by changing the fingers neatly and precisely. Untidy fingering will produce unwanted notes.

68.

doo —— doo —— doo — doo —— doo — doo —

69.

doo ———— doo ———— doo ———— doo ——

70.

doo —— doo doo — doo doo — doo doo —

71.

doo —————— doo ————— doo ———— doo — doo ——

72.

73.

Slurs will be used at appropriate places in both exercises and tunes from now on.

Time Signature

Every tune you have played has had two figures beside the Treble Clef. These two figures are known as the *Time Signature*.

The **top figure** tells you **how many beats** there are in a bar.

The **bottom figure** tells you **the value** of each beat. As **4** stands for crotchet ('quarter note') —

$\frac{2}{4}$ means two crotchet (quarter note) beats in a bar

$\frac{3}{4}$ means three crotchet (quarter note) beats in a bar

$\frac{4}{4}$ means four crotchet (quarter note) beats in a bar

What does $\frac{6}{4}$ mean?

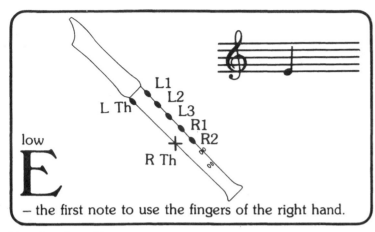

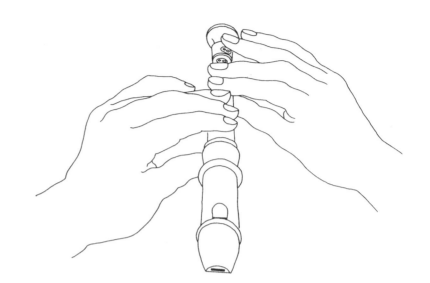

low
E

— the first note to use the fingers of the right hand.

To play low E:

1. Finger G and cover the next two holes with the first two fingers of the right hand (R1 and R2).

2. Blow and tongue *gently. Low notes need very little breath pressure.*

74.

Repeat several times

75. ☐ Football Chant

'We are the cham-pions'

76 (a)

76 (b)

Play (a) with every note tongued; and (b) slurred as marked.

77. Moderato

mf

78. Gently

79. Hey Jim along
Brightly   American

E⇌A: Take particular care to move *L3* at the same time as R1 and R2.

80.
Repeat several times, unslurred and slurred

81. Firmly

82. Gently

83. Huron Carol (part)   Huron Indian
Andante

84. Play (a) with *every note tongued*; and (b) slurred as marked.

Concert Piece No. 4 – 'Carol' – on p. 94 will give you further practice in using low E.

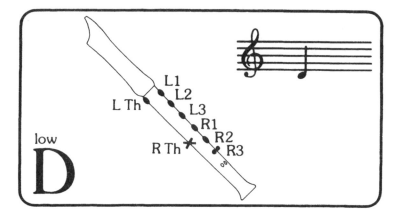

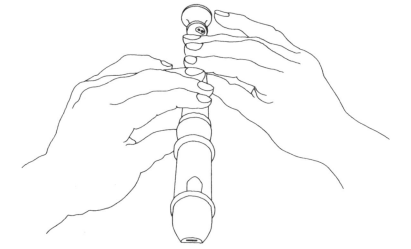

low **D**

To play low D:

1. Finger low E and add R3, pushing it well across to seal *both* small holes with the pad of the finger.

2. Blow and tongue *very* gently. You will be surprised how little breath is necessary to produce a well-nourished and in-tune low D.

The first few exercises approach low D from low E. Drop your breath pressure slightly as you prepare to tongue (*gently !*) the D.

85.

86. Turn the glasses over (part) (see No. 160)

Brightly

American

87.

Brightly

Fine

*D.C. al Fine

Compare — with — to get the rhythm correct

We are the cham-pions

* D.C. = Da Capo : from the beginning
al : to
Fine : the end
i.e. go back to the beginning and play to 'Fine'

34

D ⇄ G: is a very common move. Get used to moving all three right hand fingers *together* — like one big finger.

88. **Old Farmer Buck**
    Allegro
    English

    Meno mosso (Slower)   a tempo (back to the original speed)

89. **There were ten in the bed**
    Allegro
    English
    Fine   Dal Segno al Fine*

    −: emphasise this note   *(Go back to the sign (𝄋) and play to 'Fine')

90. **The Jolly Miller**
    Allegro
    English

D ⇄ A : pay particular attention to the L H fingers (especially L3) and make sure that
D ⇄ B   they move exactly together with the R H fingers.

91. **Chimes ('Brownie Bells')**
    Moderato

92. **Bugle Call**
    Allegro
    Fine

    D.C. al Fine
    Faster

93. **Mocking Bird**
Moderato

p cantabile (in a singing style)

American

94. **Il était un petit navire**
Allegretto

mf

French

95. **Hot Cross Buns**
Brightly

f   *mf*   *f*

English

For a complete change of style, turn now to Concert Piece No. 5 – "Square Dance" – on p. 95

A New Time Signature – $\frac{6}{8}$

So far, when the beat has divided it has divided into halves:

Such music is said to be in **simple time.**

Beats, however, can also divide into thirds and this is known as **compound time.**

The most common compound time signature is $\frac{6}{8}$ i.e. 6 quavers in a bar, divided into two groups of three , so giving two strong pulses in each bar. The pulse is now shown by a dotted crotchet ( ) since 3 quavers (½ crotchet each) = 1½ crotchets.

A very common rhythm is   Count: 1 2 3 4 5 6

Here are some well-known tunes in compound time using ; ; and , the most common rhythms.

96. **Pop goes the weasel (part)**

☐ English

Count: ①2③④5⑥ ①②③ ④5 6 ①2③④5⑥ ①2 3④5 6

97. **Boys and girls come out to play (part)**

☐ English

Count: ①2③④5⑥ ①2③ ④5⑥ ①2③④5⑥ ①2③④5 6

98. **Little Bo-peep**

English

mf

Compound Time Tunes Using Low E and D

99. **A Gaelic Lullaby**

With a gentle swing

V   (V)   Scots

p

100. **The Shepherdess**

Andante

V   French

mp

V

101. **Lord Thomas and Fair Eleanor**
Moderato

English

Canons and Rounds

So that you may enjoy playing "in parts" (i.e. players playing different notes at the same time) this book contains a number of *canons* and *rounds*, usually at the end of each section. In a *canon*, the same melody is played against itself, other players starting and ending later at a fixed distance of, say, one or two beats or bars. The numbers above the music show when the later players should start, *playing the tune from the beginning*. A *round* is an endless canon in which each part returns to the beginning to play the piece over and over (round and round) again. Be sure, then, to decide how and when you are going to stop, before you start!

102. **Round – 'London's Burning!'** **(4 part)**
Allegro

☐ English

103 (a) **Round – The Cuckoo: two versions of this well-known round**
Allegretto

☐ French

103 (b) Moderato

38

 **– The Sharp**

A sharp (♯) raises a note by a *semitone,* the smallest distance between two musical notes and the distance between any two notes, black or white, side by side on a keyboard:

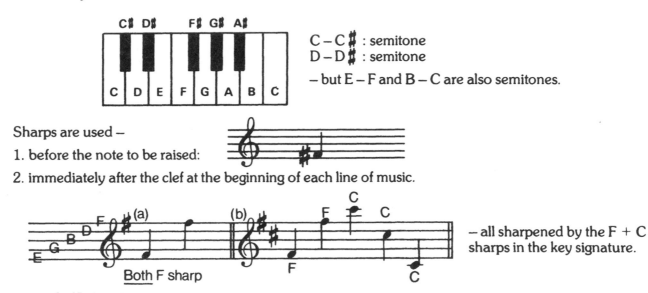

C – C♯ : semitone
D – D♯ : semitone

– but E – F and B – C are also semitones.

Sharps are used –

1. before the note to be raised:

2. immediately after the clef at the beginning of each line of music.

– all sharpened by the F + C sharps in the key signature.

Both F sharp

In (2a) as the sharp is on the line 'F', it raises *all* the Fs your instrument can play. Similarly, a second sharp in the 'C' space (2b) would raise all the Cs as well, and so on.

One to seven sharps can be used in this way and are then known as a *key signature* since they indicate in which key the piece is written. An easy way to find the name of a key from a key signature is explained in Book 2.

 **– The Natural**

A natural (♮) cancels the effect of a sharp. Although notes are usually referred to simply by their letter names, – A, B, C, etc. – it would be more correct to call them A natural, B natural, C natural etc. When raised in pitch by a sharp these notes become A sharp, B sharp, C sharp etc. A natural is then used if it is desired to lower them again to their natural form – A natural, B natural etc.

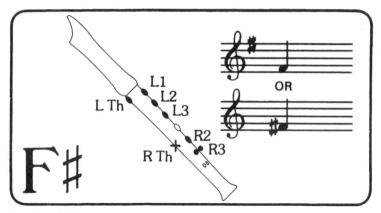

F#

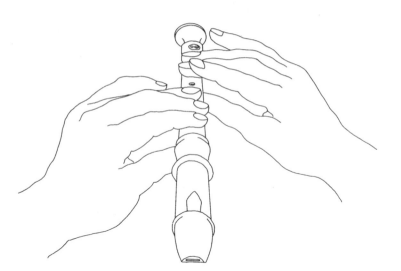

To play F#
1. Finger low D
2. Raise R1
3. Tongue and blow gently.

104. Practise slowly at first – then gradually faster:

Lift R1   Lower Lift   Lower Lift   Lower

105. In this exercise, keep your R.H. fingers over their own holes in bar 3: they may try to wander up towards your left hand!

*(Also F# – a sharp affects any other notes *of the same pitch* which *follow in the same bar.*)

106. Finger low D silently before playing to make sure that your R.H. fingers are in the correct position:

If the D in bar 4 is not too successful, your R.H. fingers may have wandered upwards again.

40

E ⇄ F♯ : Keep R2 down and let the fingers on either side see-saw round it.   Keep R2 *down* within the brackets.*

107 (a)

No. 107 (a) could also be written:

107 (b)

The sharp in the key signature (*see* P. 39) now raises *all* the Fs to F sharps.

108 (a)

With key signature:

108 (b)

Common moves using F♯

Play each many times

109.
(a)   (b)   (c)

110.   One misty, moisty morning
Brightly

mf

Herbert Wiseman

111.   Au clair de la lune
Moderato

p legato   *mp*

French

dim.: short for diminuendo:
get gradually softer

p

41

112. Happy birthday to you!
Brightly

P. S. and M. J. Hill

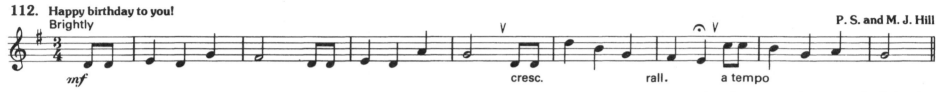

mf   cresc.   rall.   a tempo

cresc.: short for crescendo: get gradually louder

rall.: short for rallentando: get gradually slower

Five Christmas Carols

113. Good King Wençeslas

Piae Cantiones 1582

f

114. Polish Carol
Dolce (sweetly)

p   cresc.

115. My Dancing Day
Allegretto

English

mp   *mf*

mp

116. **Ding dong! merrily on high ('Branle de L'Officiel')**

Brightly

French 16C

117. **Carol of the Drum**

Moderato

Czech

*2 as the bottom figure of a time signature means *minim* (half-note).

$\frac{2}{2}$ = 2 minims (half-notes) in a bar

118. **O Waly, Waly**

Lento (slow)

English

(*3 minims (half-notes) in a bar)

119. Rigadoon
Allegro

Purcell

120. Poor Mary (Poor Jenny)
Allegretto

English

3 Compound Time Tunes

121. Here we go round the mulberry bush
Vivace (quick, lively)

English

122. The Farmer's Daughters
Vivace

English

123. Blaydon Races
Allegro

English Music Hall Song

124. Tallis' Canon (8-part)

Moderato

☐ **Thomas Tallis**

F# ⊳ A: In this move, think hard about what *L3* is doing. Make sure it moves at *exactly* the same time as your R.H. fingers.

Play Nos. 125, 126 and 127 (a) with every note tongued;
(b) slurred as shown

125. Think about L3!

126. Think about L3!

* ☐ : a minim (half note) rest.

127.

128. Michael row the boat ashore

Moderato

Negro spiritual

129. **Kum-ba-yah**
Lento

West Indian

N.B. this bar has
only 2 beats

mp

*What does 3/2 stand for?

Four More Christmas Carols

130. **D'ou viens-tu bergère**
Moderato

French-Canadian

mp (p)

(Instructions in brackets refer to the repeat)

mp

p

131. **O come, all ye faithful**
Play in
V.1 only

John Wade? 18C

f

mp

mf

* From V.2 onwards play

f

132. **Joys Seven**
Allegro

English

mf

cresc.

rall.

f

a tempo

*[1] [2] : 'first time' and 'second time' bars. The first time through the piece play the 'first time' bar and then repeat.
At the end of the repeat, *miss out the 'first time' bar* and go straight into the 'second time' bar.

46

133. I saw three ships

Allegretto

English

134. Polly Wolly Doodle

Not too fast

American

135. Drink to me only

Lento

English

136. Callino Custurame

Gently

William Byrd

137. Simple Gifts (A 'Shaker' Melody)

American

Fairly slow

mp cantabile

mf

mp

138. Bobby Shaftoe
Allegro vivace (Quick and lively)

English

mf

f

139. Dance to your daddy

British

Allegretto

rall. 2nd time

mf

f

140. The Keeper

English

Allegro

mf

Divisi (Divide (into groups) and play only your own music)

Group 1

1   1   1   1   unis. (in unison i.e. both together)

Div. (short for 'divisi')

1

mf   2   2   2   f

mf

2

Group 2

1   1   unis.

2   f

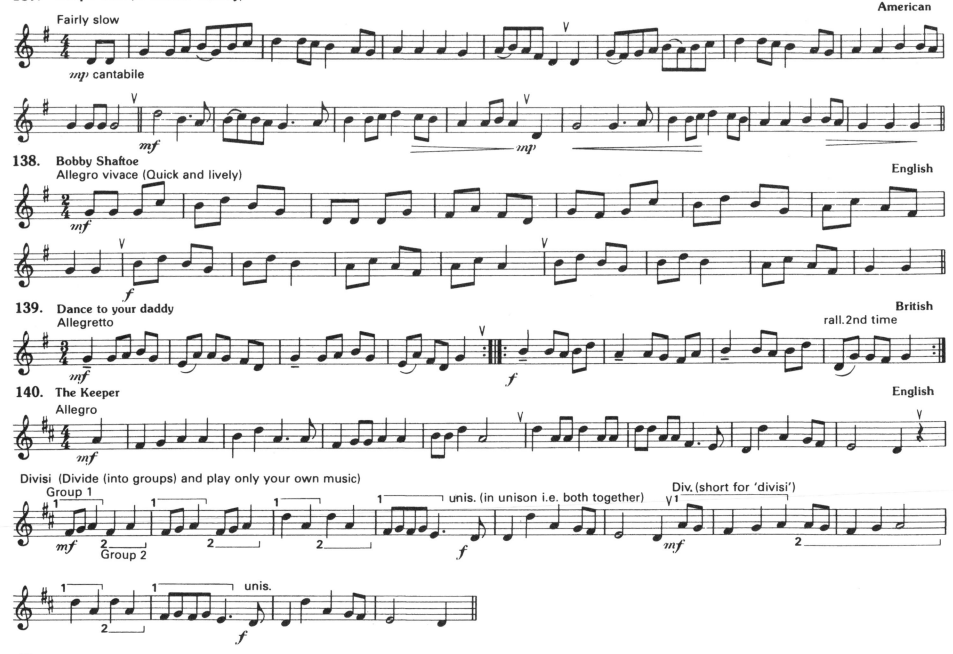

Three Rounds

141. Hark the bells (4-part)
Moderato

□ Hauptmann

142. Roses from Fyen (4-part)
Moderato

□ Danish

143. Row, row, row the boat (4-part)
Vivace

49

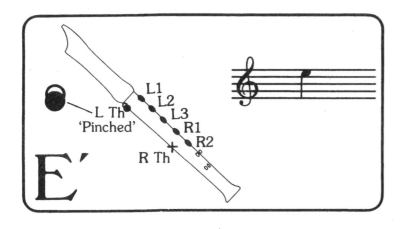

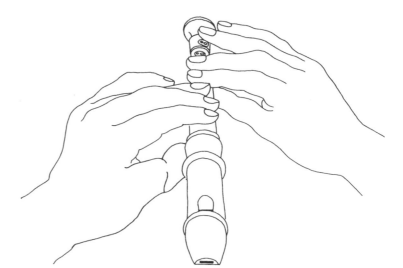

So far, the thumb has covered the thumb-hole completely or left it fully open. From E′ upwards a new and very important method of using the thumb becomes necessary in which the thumb-hole is opened only *a very small amount* (usually 3/10ths or less).

To learn this technique (commonly known as 'pinching'), play low E and gradually bend the (relaxed) thumb at the joint so that the thumb nail slips gently into the top of the thumb-hole, leaving only a tiny crescent-shaped opening above it. (See across.) If the rest of the hole is securely covered by the flesh of the thumb, the note will jump an octave (i.e. eight notes) to high E.

In moving back from the pinched to the fully covered position, the thumb-nail slides back over the upper edge of the thumb-hole (with a slight 'flick') until the hole is fully covered by the flesh again.

The length of the left thumb-nail is fairly critical. If you haven't got a left thumb-nail, grow one! Using only the flesh of the thumb for pinched notes is unreliable. Too long a nail, however, can prevent the flesh of the thumb from sealing its part of the hole adequately and must be trimmed.

Practise moving to and from the pinched position several times, playing low E and high E, slurred and tongued:-

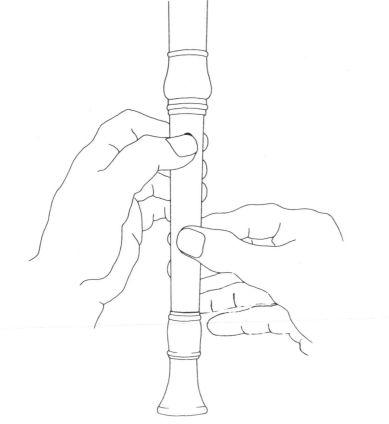

144.

Use the same breath pressure throughout.

145. Practise slowly at first; then gradually increase the speed.

146. Portsmouth (part)
Lively and rhythmic

English

147. Hymn Tune – Battishill

148. O Tannenbaum
Andante

German

149. Old Rodger is dead
Allegro

English

150. The Holly and the Ivy
Moderato

English

D′ ——▶ E′ requires special care. As the thumb is *off* for D′, it should be bent into the
'pinching' position *before* it reaches the thumbhole.

151.

152.

153.

154.

155. Allegretto

p grazioso (graceful)

156. This old man   **English**
Vivace

f

157. The National Anthem

mp

mf

f

158   All through the night

Andante

Welsh

159. Nowel's Galliard* (part)

Lively

Anon

*Galliard: a lively, triple time (i.e. 3 beats in a bar) dance, popular in the 15th and 16th centuries. Usually coupled with the Pavane (see p. 90).

160. Turn the glasses over

Brightly

American

f (but control the D's!)

161. Sweet Nightingale

With an easy swing

English

162. Il est Né — French

Moderato

163. I saw three ships — English

Brightly

164. High Germany — English

Tempo di Marcia

165. Der Schützenkönig — Praetorius

Allegro

Which tune you have already played sounds like the section marked ⌐¬?
(Answer below – upside down)

Answer: No. 64 – "La Volta".

166. **Dashing away with the smoothing iron**

Allegro vivace

English

mf

(V)

V

mf

167. **For he's a jolly good fellow** (cf. "Malbrough s'en va-t-en guerre" – French)

Vivace

English

f

rall.

V a tempo

V

V

rall.

V a tempo

168. **Round: Be you to others kind and true** (3–part)

Allegretto

☐ Jenkins

1

2

3

mp

169. **Round: The Musicians** (2–part)

Allegretto

☐ German

1

V 2

(V)

mf

A new note-value –
The Semiquaver (Sixteenth Note)

(a)  (b) Semiquaver rest

Semiquavers have double 'hooks' or tails when standing alone (a), and two *straight* tails when joined together (b). As semiquaver literally means 'half quaver', it follows that there are *two in a quaver* and *four in a crotchet*

Crotchet   1

Quavers $\frac{1}{2} + \frac{1}{2}$

Semiquavers $\frac{1}{4} + \frac{1}{4} + \frac{1}{4} + \frac{1}{4}$

The following diagram shows how some very useful rhythms come from   :

(a)   (b)   (c)

$\frac{1}{2} + \frac{1}{4} + \frac{1}{4} = 1$ $\frac{3}{4} + \frac{1}{4} = 1$ $\frac{1}{4} + \frac{1}{4} + \frac{1}{2} = 1$

Note that each rhythm takes the time of one crotchet.

The following sections give practice in using ,   and .   is not used until Book **2**.

Clap these exercises (and make up tunes to fit, if you like):

(a)

(b)

(c)

56

Some tunes using ♫♫ starting with two you have already played in longer note-values:

170. **Hot cross buns (See No. 95)**
Brightly

☐ English

171. **It's me, O Lord (See No. 26)**
Not too fast

☐ Negro Spiritual

172. **Spanish Folk Tune**

Brightly

Play with and without slurs

173. **The Rakes of Mallow (part)**
Presto (Quick)

Irish

If, when playing this tune quickly, you find it awkward to

tongue ♫♫ to "doo-doo-doo-doo", try

"doo-goo-doo-goo" instead.

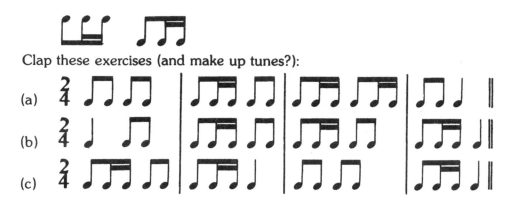

Clap these exercises (and make up tunes?):

(a)

(b)

(c)

Tunes using  , starting with a complete version of another song you have already played:

174. **The Grand Old Duke of York**

English

175. **Danish Folk Song (part)**

Gently

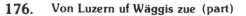

176. **Von Luzern uf Wäggis zue (part)**

Lively

Swiss

Tunes using both ♫♫ and ♫

177. **The Jolly Miller (See No. 90)**

Allegro   English

mf

178. **Mocking Bird (See No. 93)**

Moderato   American

p cantabile

Can you play the rest from memory ?

179. **J'ai du bon tabac**

Moderato   French
                                                                                                        D.C. al Fine

mp   Fine V

mf

180. **Since we are met**

Allegretto   English

mf   f   mf   f

181. **From the Overture "William Tell"**

Presto   Rossini

                                        (V) (for slow practice only)

f

*Tongue doo-goo|doo doo-goo doo doo-goo|doo doo doo etc.

doo-goo-doo - - goo-doo-goo

The long first note and the short second make a jerky, lively rhythm, much used in marching tunes. "John Brown's Body" (p. 82) will remind you of how it sounds:

John Brown's body lies a-mould'ring in the grave

Clap the rhythm of the line, then play it using only the note G. A useful dodge to keep the rhythm lively is to tongue the final semi-quaver of ♪ as *late* as you dare. (But not *too* late!)

The next few tunes will give your tongue plenty of practice.

182. If you're happy

Lively

American

183. The Quartermaster's Store

Tempo di marcia

English

Più (more) legato

184. Three Craws (Crows)

Brightly

Scots

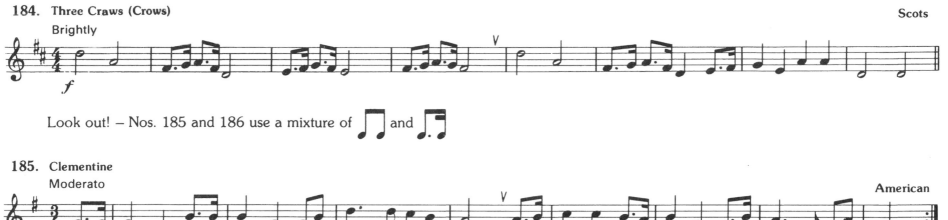

Look out! – Nos. 185 and 186 use a mixture of  and

185. Clementine

Moderato

American

186. Trek Song

Allegro

South African

The next two tunes use all three rhythms –

187. The British Grenadiers

Tempo di marcia

English

188. Camptown Races

Lively

Stephen Foster

① and ② and ① and ② and

*doo-goo-doo-goo tonguings here

Played neatly at the proper speed, No. 189 "Tambourin" and Concert Piece No. 6, "Polka Dots", on p. 96 will clearly show how well you can cope with all you have learned so far. As always, start learning both pieces at a comfortable pace and *gradually* build up speed.

189. Tambourin

Very rhythmic, but not too fast

French

Fine

D.C. al Fine

Just as in $\frac{3}{4}$ time (3 crotchets in a bar) the crotchets may divide into quavers –

Dance to your daddy (See No. 139)
Allegretto

so in $\frac{3}{8}$ time (3 quavers in a bar) the quavers may divide into semiquavers.

The last movement of **Sonata No. 8 in G** by **Robert Valentine** (c. 1730)* shows this clearly. Count silently throughout:

190. Allegro

*Edited Lefkovitch and Bergmann.
Schott Series 33.
(Trills have been omitted at ✱)

Semiquavers in Compound Time

In $\frac{6}{8}$ time, especially in song tunes, the sixth and last quaver of the bar frequently divides into semiquavers:

191. Under the Greenwood Tree
Allegro

English

ritard. (get gradually slower)

(See also Nos. 193 & 195)

192. **Floating down the river (part)**

With a gentle swing

American

mf

① ② 3 4 5 ⑥

① ②3 4 5 ⑥ and

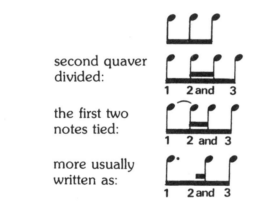

Of course *any* quaver can be divided and this very useful and graceful rhythm
results from dividing the second quaver of each group of three.

second quaver
divided:

1   2 and   3

the first two
notes tied:

1   2 and   3

more usually
written as:

1   2 and   3

193. **Skye Boat Song**

A. C. MacLeod

With a slow swing

Fine

mp ①2and③ ④5 ⑥and

D.C. al Fine

f

64

194. Sellenger's Round
Allegro

William Byrd

195. The Meeting of the Waters
Moderato

Irish

* get a little slower

196. Ye Banks and Braes
Moderato

Scots

* Here the last quaver of ♩.♪♪ is also divided:

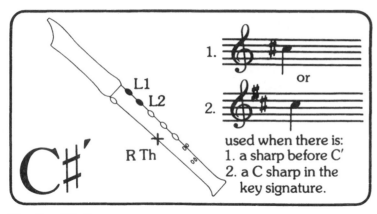

C#′

L1
L2
R Th

1. [notation]
   or
2. [notation]

used when there is:
1. a sharp before C′
2. a C sharp in the key signature.

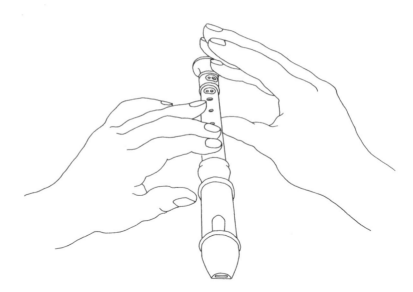

To play C′ sharp:

1. Finger A and take off the left thumb (*not too far*).

2. Blow and tongue gently. C♯′ goes out of tune easily.

197. Note the C♯ in the key signature!

Play (a) without slurs (b) with slurs.

*In moving from B ⇌ C♯′, L1 stays down as a pivot for the hand to rock round.

198.

199.

200.

201. With a gentle swing

mp grazioso

202. "His Humour" (part)

Allegretto

Giles Farnaby

*The signs in brackets are friendly reminders!

203. 'Now is the month of Maying'

Brightly

Thomas Morley

204. Carol of the Birds

Gently

Czech

(break without taking a breath)

205. 'Yellow Bird'

Moderato

Haitian

206. 'Unto us a Boy is born'

Allegro ma non troppo (Fast but not too fast)

Piae Cantiones 1582

207. **Old Zip Coon**

The Scale* of D major (* from the Latin 'Scala' – a ladder)

208 (a)

Two ways of varying this scale:

208 (b)

208 (c)

The Arpeggio* of D major

(* from the Italian 'Arpeggiare' — to play like a harp. Can you think why?)

209 (a)   **209 (b)**

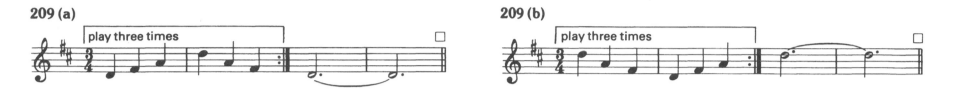

Play scales and arpeggios evenly and rhythmically *and only as fast as you can play the most difficult finger changes cleanly and correctly.* Start by practising slowly and then build up speed very gradually.

We shall meet more and more scales and arpeggios from now on. Get into the habit of playing a *few every day.*

210.

211.

212. Helston Furry Dance

69

213. 'Ho-la-hi'

Allegro

German

214. 'Tzena Tzena' (May be played as a 2-part round)

Presto

Israeli

215. 'The old woman and the pedlar'

Moderato

English

216. Can-Can (from 'Orpheus in the Underworld')

As fast as possible! – and all on one breath!

Offenbach

217. Tinga Layo

Moderato

West Indian

218. Advent Carol ('People look east')

Brightly

French

219. Round: Lullaby (9-part)

Moderato

□ Anon

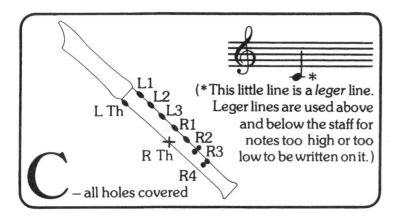

C — all holes covered

(*This little line is a *leger* line. Leger lines are used above and below the staff for notes too high or too low to be written on it.)

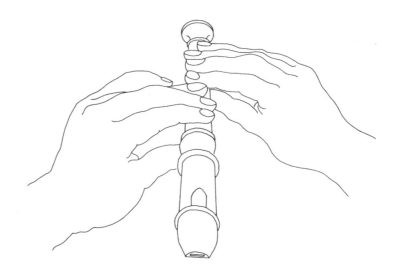

To play low C:

1. If your recorder is made in three sections twist the end-joint round until the double-hole lies comfortably under the right little finger. Because this finger is so short, the double hole will be out of line with the others and well over to your right.

2. Finger low D and add R4. Keep the *third* fingers of both hands pushed well across. Now, with all holes covered, blow and tongue very gently. Try tonguing with a *soft* 'd' sound. The merest wisp of breath will produce a good, round C. Learn to control this amount of breath by tonguing bottom C several times in succession.

220. In the following tunes, gradually drop your breath pressure as you approach low E, D and C.

221.

Slur both ways

(a)
(b)

222.

223.

224. We wish you a Merry Christmas

Brightly   English

f

225. The Cherry Tree Carol

Allegretto   English

mf cantabile

226. Maa Bonny Lad

Not too fast   English

mp

227. Bunessan

Gently   Gaelic

p legato

*$\frac{9}{4}$: 9 crotchets in a bar in 3 groups of 3 (see dotted lines)

228. Swanee River (part)

Andante   Stephen Foster

229. Sweet England

Moderato   English

230. The Seeds of Love

Andante   English

231. Over the hills and far away

Allegro   English

232. The Barnyard Song

Moderato

American

* Semiquaver rest – see p.56

233. Shortnin' Bread

With an easy swing

American

234. The Day we went to Rothesay ("The Tinkler's Weddin' ")

With bounce

Scots

235. Round: "Mark where the bee" (3-part)

Moderato

□ Anon

236 Round: "Fair morn" (3-part)

□ Anon

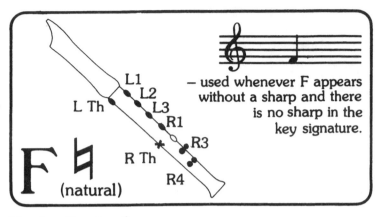

F ♮
(natural)

L Th — L1 L2 L3 R1 R3 R Th R4

– used whenever F appears without a sharp and there is no sharp in the key signature.

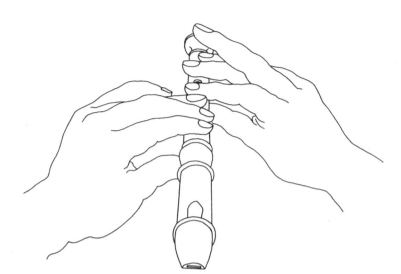

To play F natural:

1. Finger low C and raise R2 (the *middle* finger of the right hand).

2. Blow and tongue gently.

3. Now practise raising and lowering R2 while the other fingers stay down. Blow gently and continuously:

237.

etc

Make sure that R4 seals both small holes properly: *otherwise F will be out of tune.*

238.

239. R1 and 3 stay down within the bracket.

F ⇄ E –a finger change which needs a lot of practice. Think hard about the outgoing fingers and practise until all unwanted notes disappear.

240.

241 (a)

Is R4 still sealing properly?

241 (b) The slurs will show up any untidy fingering.

242.

F ⇄ D – R1 and 3 stay down: R2 and 4 rock around R3.
243.

R1 and 3 down within brackets.

244. 'Past Three o'clock' (part)

Andante

English

mf

R1 and 3 down

F⇄G – Finger F and raise and lower the right hand fingers *as a unit* – i.e. keeping R2 raised about half-an-inch above the others throughout. Lift the fingers straight up and keep them *immediately above* their holes *even when not in use. This is very important.*

245.

Keep R H fingers in F position

246.

Keep R H in F position throughout

Tunes using all these shifts

247. Moderato

mf

248. Start by practising:

Repeat each many times

The Scale of C

249 (a)

249 (b)

Variants

249 (c)

249 (d)

Arpeggio of C

250 (a)

play three times

250 (b)

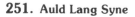

play three times

251. Auld Lang Syne

Moderato

Scots

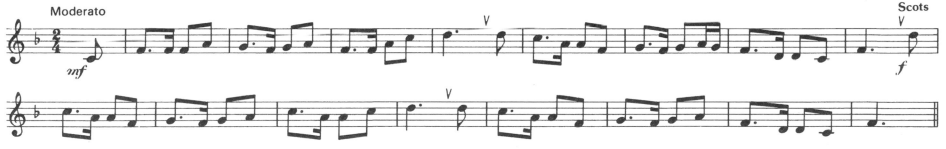

mf   f

252. Hullabaloo Balay

Briskly

Sea Shanty

f

79

253. Soldier, Soldier

Allegretto

English

254. Jennie Jenkins

Moderato

American

255. Goodbye Old Paint

American Cowboy Song

Andante

Fine

(V)

D.C. al Fine
(with repeat)

256. A la claire Fontaine

French Canadian

Moderato

257. Carman's Whistle

William Byrd

Rhythmic – but not too fast

Careful! ① ② 3 ④ ⑤ 6   ① ② 3 ④ 5 ⑥

258. Mein Freund

Stately

Susato

mp legato

rall. 2nd time

259. John Barleycorn

Briskly

English

f

260. We shall overcome

Moderato

Horton/Hamilton/Carawan/Seeger

mf

mf

261. John Brown's Body

Tempo di marcia

American

mf

* *f*

often played

262. Tramp, tramp, tramp (rhythm slightly altered)

G.F. Root

Tempo di marcia

mf

f

The next tune uses both F♯ and F♮. Play F♯ only where marked. All other Fs are F naturals.

263. There is a Tavern in the Town

Allegro

English

mf

82

264. Round: `Wacht auf!` (2-part)

265. Round: `Hark I hear the hunters' hollo` (3-part)

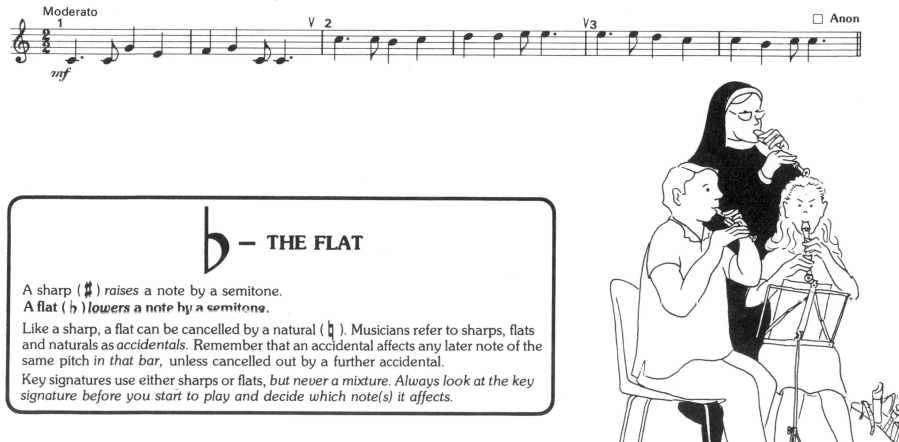

♭ – THE FLAT

A sharp (♯) *raises* a note by a semitone.
A flat (♭) *lowers* a note by a semitone.

Like a sharp, a flat can be cancelled by a natural (♮). Musicians refer to sharps, flats and naturals as *accidentals.* Remember that an accidental affects any later note of the same pitch *in that bar,* unless cancelled out by a further accidental.

Key signatures use either sharps or flats, *but never a mixture. Always look at the key signature before you start to play and decide which note(s) it affects.*

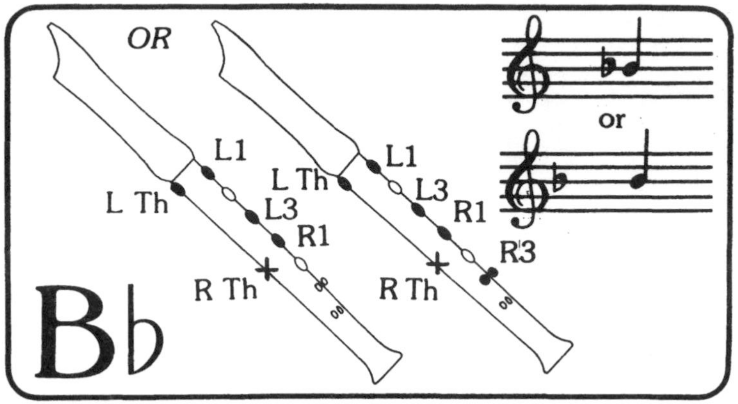

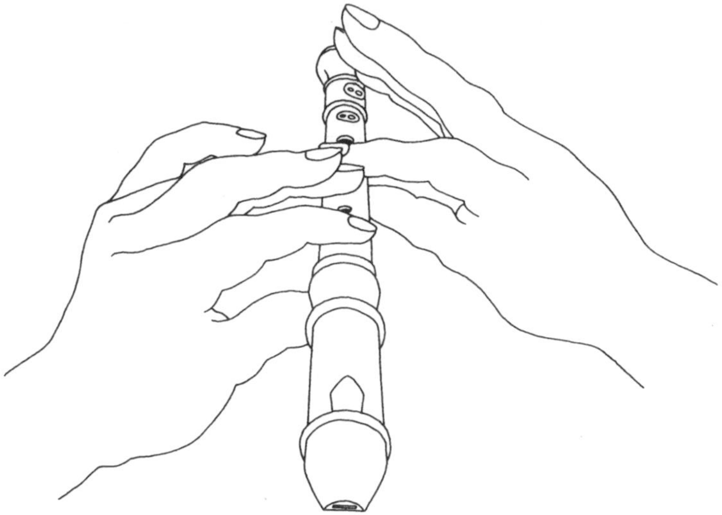

To play B♭:

1. Finger G and raise L2 (the *middle* finger). Add R1. Blow and tongue. This is the usual fingering.
2. On some recorders, B♭ is better in tune with R3 added to the usual fingering. If in doubt, seek advice.
3. Whichever fingering is used, *both hands must lift and lower absolutely together.*

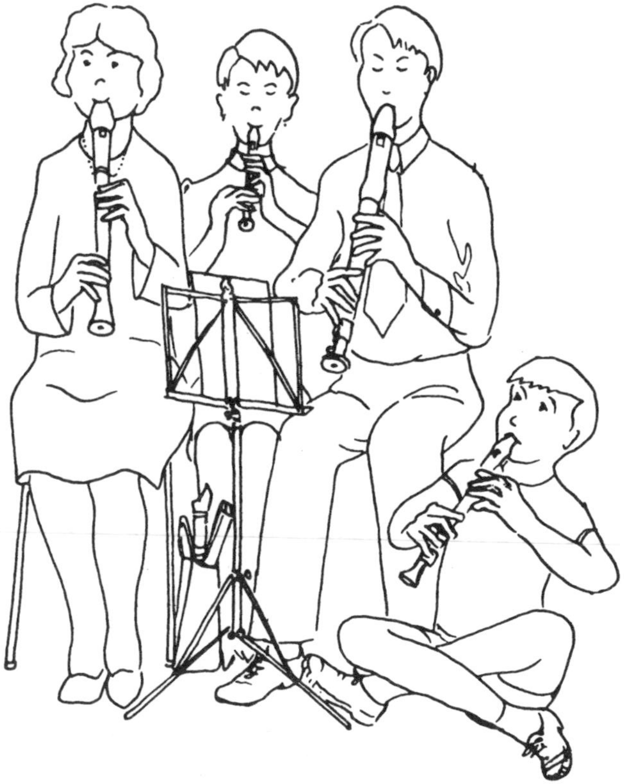

Practise Exs. 266 and 267 regularly, first unslurred and then slurred, until all unwanted sounds disappear.

266. Look at the key signature! What is the name of the first note?

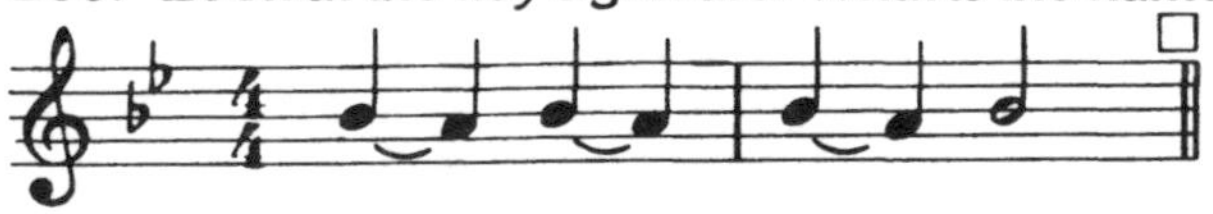

267.

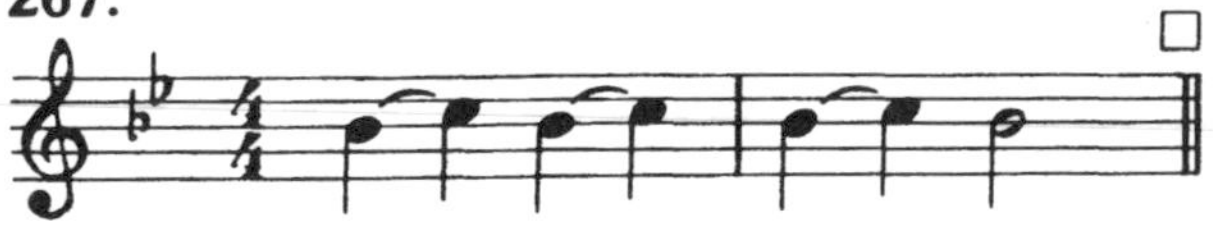

268.

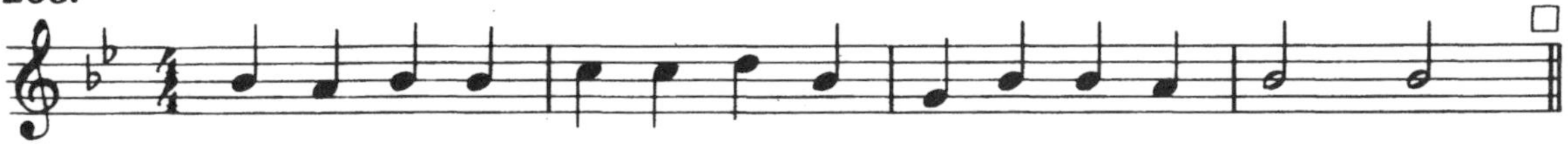

269 (a)

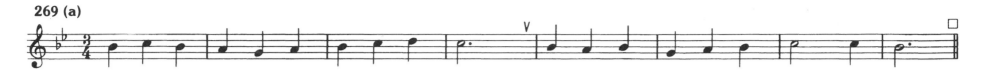

269 (b)

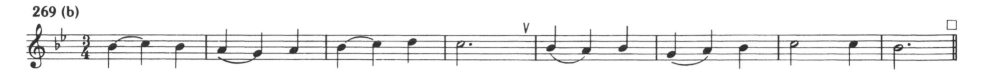

270.

Allegretto grazioso

mp

271.

272.

273.

274.

275.

276. Quem Pastores

With a gentle swing

German 14C

p grazioso

(V)

277. While shepherds watched (Tune: Winchester Old)

English

mf

278. Johnny Todd

Moderato

English

f

279. Hark! the herald angels sing

Mendelssohn

f

280. Rocking

Gently

Czech

281. Fire Down Below!

Briskly

Sea Shanty

282. The Tailor and the Mouse

Allegro giocoso (Fast and merry)

English

283. Crimond (23rd Psalm)

Andante

Jessie Irvine
(v.1 only)

(not v.1)

(not v.1)

One more river

Lively

American

285. **My Bonnie lies over the ocean**

Tempo di valse (in waltz time)

American

rall.   à tempo

286. **Begone, dull care ("The Queen's Jig" C.1700)**

Briskly

English

287. Ronde – "Wo bistu"

288. Ronde

rit. 2nd time only

289. Königstanz

290. Parson's Farewell

291. Pavane*

Slow and stately

Arbeau

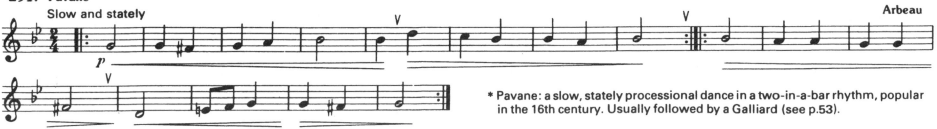

p

* Pavane: a slow, stately processional dance in a two-in-a-bar rhythm, popular in the 16th century. Usually followed by a Galliard (see p.53).

292. Pat-a-pan

Tempo di marcia

French

f

293. Round: O how lovely is the evening (3-part)

With a gentle swing

German

p

294. Round: Music shall live (3-part)(a variant of No. 169)

Moderato

Danish

mf

WHAT NEXT?

If you have mastered all the notes, rhythms and musical signs in this book you will now be able to play literally thousands of tunes. But your recorder is capable of many more notes yet and **"ENJOY THE RECORDER" Book 2** will teach you these and introduce you to more fine music of all kinds. You will have found already that the more you learn about the recorder and its music the more enjoyable playing it becomes, so do press on into Book 2.

See you then!

SIX CONCERT PIECES

No. 1
'DRIFTING ALONG'

* A treble clef with a tiny 8 above it is often used in descant recorder music to show that the descant sounds an octave (i.e. eight notes) above the printed notes – something you may not have realised.

✲ When Nos: 68-73 have been mastered, slurs may be used where shown.

No. 2
MARCH

Brian Bonsor

poco rit. (get a little slower)

BEGINNERS' BEGUINE

Tempo di Beguine (In Beguine time)

Brian Bonsor

Descant

f (* omit in descant only version)

Optional treble and/or tuned percussion

(2nd time)

*1. (First time)   2. (Second time)

divisi ⊛

* for explanation see No. 132.

⊛ "divided" – into 3 in descants only and descants/percussion versions.
– into 2 when trebles play, omitting descant 'G'

93

CAROL

Brian Bonsor

dim. - - - - - - - - - - e- - - - - - rit.
(get gradually softer and slower)

pp
(very soft)

No. 5

SQUARE DANCE

Brian Bonsor

No. 6

POLKA DOTS

Descants I & II : When 'divisi' – I: play notes with stems up
II: play notes with stems down

Brian Bonsor

Alla (in the manner of a) Polka

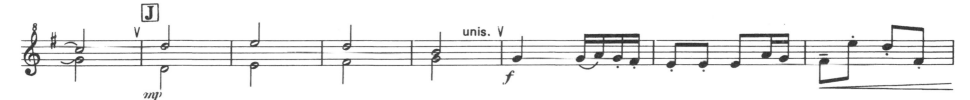

* Divide into 3 groups

ITALIAN TERMS

Dynamics (degrees of loudness and softness)

f (forte): loud
p (piano): soft
m (mezzo): medium; moderately
mf (mezzo forte): moderately loud
mp (mezzo piano): moderately soft
ff (fortissimo): very loud
pp (pianissimo): very soft

crescendo
cresc. > : get gradually louder

diminuendo
dim. > : get gradually softer

Speeds

Allegro: lively, quick
Allegretto: fairly lively (but less so than Allegro)
Andante: at a moderate (walking) pace
a tempo: back to the original time
Lento: slow
Meno mosso: less movement i.e. slower
Moderato: at a moderate speed
Mosso: moved, movement
Presto: quick

Rallentando (rall.): gradually slower
Ritardando (ritard.): gradually slower
Tempo di beguine: in beguine time
Tempo di marcia: in march time
Tempo di valse: in waltz time
Vivace: vivacious, quick, lively

ma non troppo: but not too much
meno: less – as in 'meno mosso': less movement i.e. slower
molto: much, very – as in 'molto rall.': get gradually much slower; 'molto vivace': very quickly
più: more – as in 'più mosso': more movement i.e. quicker
poco: a little – as in 'poco ritard.': get a little slower gradually
e, ed: and – as in 'dim. e ritard.': get gradually softer and slower

Descriptive terms

Alla: in the manner of
Cantabile: in a singing style
Dolce: sweet
Giocoso: gay, merry
Grazioso: graceful
Legato: smooth
Staccato: detached

Musical Signs

< : **crescendo:** get gradually louder

> : **diminuendo:** get gradually softer

⌒ : pause

– : emphasis

𝄋 : the sign (Segno)

Da Capo (D.C.): From the beginning

Dal Segno (D.S. or D.𝄋): From the sign 𝄋

(al) Fine: (to) the end

┌1.──── : ‖ ┌2.──── : first and second time bars – see No. 132

‖: :‖ : repeat – see page 18

, : make a break

divisi: divided
div.

unis.: together

INDEX OF TUNES

* Christmas carols and songs
° Rounds

Acknowledgements

The author and publisher are grateful to the following who have allowed copyright material to be used in this book:

Essex Music Ltd.   We Shall Overcome
by Horton, Hamilton, Carawan, and Seeger.

Frank Music Co. Ltd.   Yellow Bird
by Norman Luboff
©1957 Walton Music Corporation

Keith Prowse Music   Happy Birthday to You
Publishing Co. Ltd.   by Patty and Mildred Hill
©1939

Oxford University Press One Misty, Moisty Morning
by Herbert Wiseman
from Sixty Songs for Little Children